OHETA SOPHIA

Future of Mental Health Care: Innovations and Trends

Copyright © 2024 by OHETA SOPHIA

All rights reserved. No part of this publication may be reproduced, stored or transmitted in any form or by any means, electronic, mechanical, photocopying, recording, scanning, or otherwise without written permission from the publisher. It is illegal to copy this book, post it to a website, or distribute it by any other means without permission.

OHETA SOPHIA asserts the moral right to be identified as the author of this work.

OHETA SOPHIA has no responsibility for the persistence or accuracy of URLs for external or third-party Internet Websites referred to in this publication and does not guarantee that any content on such Websites is, or will remain, accurate or appropriate.

Designations used by companies to distinguish their products are often claimed as trademarks. All brand names and product names used in this book and on its cover are trade names, service marks, trademarks and registered trademarks of their respective owners. The publishers and the book are not associated with any product or vendor mentioned in this book. None of the companies referenced within the book have endorsed the book.

First edition

This book was professionally typeset on Reedsy.
Find out more at reedsy.com

Contents

1	Introduction to the Future of Mental Health Care	1
2	Technological Advances in Mental Health	5
3	The Role of Personalized Medicine	9
4	Integration of Mental and Physical Health Care	13
5	Innovations in Psychotherapy and Counseling	17
6	The Impact of Social Media on Mental Health	22
7	The Future of Mental Health Care: Emerging Trends and...	26
8	Mental Health and the Workplace: Emerging Strategies for...	31
9	The Role of Community in Mental Health: Building Supportive...	35
10	Epilogue: Embracing the Future of Mental Health Care	39

1

Introduction to the Future of Mental Health Care

The field of mental health care is on the cusp of a transformative era. As we stand at the intersection of technological advancement, evolving societal attitudes, and an increased understanding of mental health, it is crucial to explore what the future holds for this essential aspect of healthcare. This chapter provides a comprehensive overview of the current state of mental health care, the driving forces behind its evolution, and the key trends that are likely to shape its future.

Mental health care, traditionally characterized by face-to-face consultations, limited access, and often a reactive approach, is undergoing a significant shift. The last few decades have seen gradual improvements in awareness and treatment, but these changes are now accelerating due to technological advancements and changing societal expectations. The need for innovation in mental health care stems from several pressing challenges: the rising prevalence of mental health conditions, disparities in access to care, and the limitations of existing treatment models.

One of the most prominent drivers of change in mental health care is the rapid advancement of technology. Digital health tools, such as teletherapy platforms and mental health apps, are becoming increasingly integrated into the fabric of mental health care. These tools have expanded access to care, especially for individuals in remote or underserved areas, and have made it possible to offer support in a more flexible and personalized manner. Teletherapy, for example, allows individuals to connect with mental health professionals from the comfort of their homes, reducing barriers related to transportation, time constraints, and stigma.

The rise of artificial intelligence (AI) and machine learning is another significant trend influencing the future of mental health care. AI-powered tools are being developed to assist in diagnosis, predict treatment outcomes, and provide personalized recommendations. Machine learning algorithms can analyze vast amounts of data to identify patterns and trends that may not be apparent to human clinicians. This capability has the potential to enhance diagnostic accuracy, optimize treatment plans, and ultimately improve patient outcomes. Additionally, AI-driven chatbots and virtual assistants are being used to provide immediate support and guidance, further expanding the reach and accessibility of mental health resources.

Personalized medicine, which tailors treatment to the individual based on their unique genetic, environmental, and lifestyle factors, is gaining traction in the field of mental health. Advances in genomics and neuroscience are paving the way for more customized approaches to treatment. For instance, pharmacogenomics, the study of how genes affect a person's response to medications, is helping to develop more effective and targeted psychotropic drugs. Personalized therapy approaches that consider an individual's specific needs and preferences are also being explored, allowing for more precise and effective interventions.

Another critical trend shaping the future of mental health care is the integration of mental and physical health care. Traditionally, mental health and physical health have been treated as separate entities, but there is growing recognition of the interconnectedness between them. Integrative care models that address both mental and physical health are being developed to provide more comprehensive and holistic care. These models often involve multidisciplinary teams that include mental health professionals, primary care providers, and specialists working collaboratively to address the full spectrum of a patient's needs.

The evolving landscape of psychotherapeutic approaches is also noteworthy. Innovations in psychotherapy, such as the use of virtual reality (VR) and immersive technologies, are offering new ways to address mental health conditions. VR can create controlled environments for exposure therapy, allowing patients to confront and manage fears and anxieties in a safe and monitored setting. Additionally, new therapeutic modalities, such as online cognitive-behavioral therapy (CBT) programs, are providing alternative and accessible options for individuals seeking mental health support.

Social media and online communities are playing an increasingly significant role in mental health care. On one hand, social media platforms provide opportunities for individuals to share experiences, seek support, and connect with others who may be facing similar challenges. On the other hand, there are concerns about the impact of social media on mental health, including issues related to cyberbullying, comparison, and screen time. Understanding the dual role of social media in mental health is crucial for developing effective strategies to harness its benefits while mitigating its risks.

As mental health care continues to evolve, so too must the policies and frameworks that govern it. The future of mental health policy will likely involve a focus on ensuring equitable access to care, addressing disparities in service delivery, and adapting regulations to accommodate new technologies and treatment approaches. Advocacy and policy changes will be essential in shaping a mental health care system that is inclusive, effective, and responsive to the needs of diverse populations.

Education and training for mental health professionals are also adapting to these changes. The integration of new technologies, therapies, and approaches requires ongoing professional development and education. Future mental health practitioners will need to be adept in using digital tools, understanding new treatment modalities, and navigating the complexities of integrated care models.

Ethical considerations are central to the future of mental health care. As technology advances and new treatments emerge, questions about privacy, consent, and the equitable distribution of resources will become increasingly important. Ensuring that innovations in mental health care are implemented in a way that respects individual rights and promotes fairness will be a critical challenge.

In conclusion, the future of mental health care is poised to be shaped by a convergence of technological advancements, evolving therapeutic approaches, and a growing emphasis on holistic and personalized care. The trends discussed in this chapter highlight the potential for a more accessible, effective, and integrated mental health care system. As we navigate these changes, it will be essential to remain mindful of the ethical implications and strive for a system that meets the diverse needs of individuals while promoting overall well-being. The subsequent chapters will delve deeper into these trends, exploring their implications and potential for transforming mental health care in the years to come.

2

Technological Advances in Mental Health

In recent years, technological advancements have made significant inroads into various aspects of healthcare, and mental health care is no exception. The integration of technology into mental health services is revolutionizing how care is delivered, making it more accessible, personalized, and efficient. This chapter explores the major technological innovations transforming mental health care, including teletherapy, digital mental health apps, and the use of artificial intelligence (AI) and machine learning.

Teletherapy, also known as online therapy or virtual therapy, represents one of the most significant advancements in mental health care. The concept of teletherapy involves providing therapeutic services through digital platforms such as video conferencing, phone calls, or chat-based applications. This approach has several advantages, including increased accessibility for individuals who may have difficulty attending in-person sessions due to geographical, physical, or logistical barriers. Teletherapy has proven particularly valuable during crises like the COVID-19 pandemic, which necessitated social distancing and limited in-person interactions. It allowed therapists to continue providing care while adhering to public health guidelines.

The rise of teletherapy is accompanied by the development of various digital platforms designed to facilitate remote mental health services. These platforms often feature secure video conferencing tools, electronic health records, and communication channels that enable therapists to conduct sessions, track progress, and manage patient information efficiently. The convenience and flexibility of teletherapy have made it a popular choice for many individuals seeking mental health support. It also offers the potential for expanded access to specialists who may not be available locally, thereby reducing disparities in mental health care access.

Digital mental health apps represent another major innovation in the field. These apps provide a wide range of services, from self-help resources and mood tracking to guided meditation and cognitive-behavioral therapy (CBT) exercises. Apps like Headspace, Calm, and Moodfit offer users tools to manage stress, anxiety, and depression, often incorporating features such as daily reminders, interactive exercises, and progress tracking. The widespread adoption of smartphones and wearable technology has facilitated the growth of these apps, making mental health support more readily available to individuals at their fingertips.

The development of mental health apps also includes specialized applications designed to address specific conditions or demographics. For example, apps tailored for adolescents or young adults may focus on issues related to school stress, social media pressures, or peer relationships. Similarly, apps designed for individuals with chronic mental health conditions, such as bipolar disorder or schizophrenia, may include features for tracking symptoms, medication adherence, and providing educational resources. These specialized apps aim to provide targeted support and enhance the overall effectiveness of mental health care.

Artificial intelligence (AI) and machine learning are rapidly becoming integral components of mental health care. AI encompasses a range of technologies that enable machines to perform tasks that typically require human intelligence, such as analyzing data, recognizing patterns, and making decisions.

In the context of mental health, AI is being utilized to improve diagnostic accuracy, personalize treatment plans, and enhance patient engagement.

One notable application of AI in mental health is the development of algorithms that can analyze speech and text to detect signs of mental health conditions. For instance, AI tools can analyze language patterns, tone of voice, and speech rate to identify potential symptoms of depression, anxiety, or psychosis. These tools can assist clinicians in making more accurate diagnoses and providing timely interventions. Additionally, AI-powered chatbots and virtual assistants are being used to offer immediate support, provide psychoeducation, and guide users through therapeutic exercises. These AI-driven tools can complement traditional therapy by offering additional resources and support outside of regular sessions.

Machine learning, a subset of AI that involves training algorithms to recognize patterns and make predictions based on data, is also playing a role in mental health care. Machine learning models can analyze large datasets to identify trends and predict treatment outcomes, enabling more personalized and effective interventions. For example, machine learning algorithms can analyze data from electronic health records, genetic information, and behavioral assessments to develop individualized treatment plans and predict responses to different therapies.

Another area of technological innovation in mental health care is the use of virtual reality (VR) and augmented reality (AR). VR creates immersive environments that can be used for therapeutic purposes, such as exposure therapy for phobias or post-traumatic stress disorder (PTSD). AR, on the other hand, overlays digital information onto the real world, which can be used to enhance therapeutic experiences and provide interactive interventions. Both VR and AR offer new ways to engage patients in their treatment and provide immersive experiences that may be more effective than traditional methods.

The integration of technology into mental health care also raises important considerations regarding data security and privacy. As mental health services become increasingly digital, protecting patient information becomes paramount. Ensuring that digital platforms comply with regulations such as the Health Insurance Portability and Accountability Act (HIPAA) and implementing robust security measures are essential to safeguarding sensitive data and maintaining patient trust.

In conclusion, technological advances are reshaping the landscape of mental health care, offering new opportunities for enhancing accessibility, personalization, and effectiveness. Teletherapy, digital mental health apps, AI, and emerging technologies like VR and AR are transforming how mental health services are delivered and experienced. As these technologies continue to evolve, they hold the promise of further improving mental health care and addressing the diverse needs of individuals. However, it is crucial to address the associated challenges, such as data security and privacy concerns, to ensure that these innovations are implemented in a manner that prioritizes patient well-being and maintains the highest standards of care.

3

The Role of Personalized Medicine

Personalized medicine is revolutionizing the landscape of healthcare by tailoring treatments to individual patients based on their unique genetic, environmental, and lifestyle factors. This approach, which aims to provide more precise and effective interventions, is particularly impactful in the field of mental health care. This chapter delves into the various dimensions of personalized medicine in mental health, exploring how advancements in genomics, neuroscience, and data analytics are shaping more individualized treatment strategies and improving patient outcomes.

At the heart of personalized medicine is the use of genetic information to inform treatment decisions. Genomics, the study of an individual's complete set of genes and their interactions, has opened new avenues for understanding and addressing mental health conditions. By analyzing genetic variations, researchers can identify biomarkers associated with different mental health disorders, such as depression, bipolar disorder, and schizophrenia. These biomarkers can provide insights into an individual's risk of developing a condition, as well as their likely response to various treatments.

For example, pharmacogenomics is a field within personalized medicine that focuses on how genetic differences affect an individual's response to medications. In the context of mental health, pharmacogenomic testing can help determine which antidepressants or antipsychotics are most likely to be effective for a particular patient. This approach reduces the trial-and-error process often associated with finding the right medication and minimizes the risk of adverse effects. By tailoring pharmacological treatments to an individual's genetic profile, healthcare providers can enhance treatment efficacy and improve overall patient satisfaction.

In addition to genetic factors, personalized medicine in mental health also considers environmental and lifestyle influences. Epigenetics, the study of how environmental factors can alter gene expression, plays a crucial role in understanding how external factors contribute to mental health conditions. For instance, exposure to chronic stress, trauma, or substance abuse can influence gene expression and increase susceptibility to mental health disorders. By integrating environmental and lifestyle data with genetic information, personalized medicine can offer a more comprehensive understanding of mental health and inform targeted interventions.

Neuroscience has also contributed significantly to the development of personalized medicine in mental health. Advances in neuroimaging technologies, such as functional magnetic resonance imaging (fMRI) and positron emission tomography (PET), allow for detailed visualization of brain activity and structure. These technologies help identify neural patterns and abnormalities associated with various mental health conditions. For example, fMRI studies have revealed distinct brain activation patterns in individuals with depression, anxiety, or schizophrenia, which can guide the development of personalized treatment approaches.

Furthermore, the integration of data analytics and artificial intelligence (AI) is enhancing the field of personalized medicine. Machine learning algorithms can analyze large datasets, including genetic information, clinical records, and neuroimaging data, to identify patterns and predict treatment outcomes. These algorithms can assist in developing individualized treatment plans by integrating diverse data sources and providing actionable insights. For example, AI-driven models can predict how a patient might respond to different therapeutic interventions based on their unique profile, enabling more informed decision-making.

The application of personalized medicine in mental health extends beyond medication and treatment planning. It also encompasses personalized psychotherapy approaches, such as cognitive-behavioral therapy (CBT) and other therapeutic modalities. Personalized psychotherapy involves tailoring therapeutic interventions to an individual's specific needs, preferences, and goals. For example, therapy can be adapted based on factors such as the individual's cognitive style, coping strategies, and social support network. By personalizing the therapeutic process, mental health professionals can enhance engagement and effectiveness, ultimately leading to better outcomes for patients.

One of the challenges of implementing personalized medicine in mental health is ensuring equitable access to advanced diagnostics and treatments. While personalized medicine holds great promise, the availability of genetic testing, neuroimaging technologies, and AI-driven tools can vary depending on geographic location, socioeconomic status, and healthcare infrastructure. Addressing these disparities and ensuring that personalized medicine benefits are accessible to all individuals is a critical consideration for the future of mental health care.

Ethical considerations also play a significant role in the implementation of personalized medicine. Issues related to genetic privacy, data security, and informed consent must be carefully managed to protect patient rights and maintain trust. As personalized medicine involves the collection and analysis of sensitive genetic and personal information, it is essential to establish robust safeguards to ensure that this information is used responsibly and with respect for patient autonomy.

In conclusion, personalized medicine is transforming mental health care by offering more precise and individualized approaches to diagnosis, treatment, and therapy. Advances in genomics, neuroscience, and data analytics are enabling healthcare providers to tailor interventions based on an individual's unique genetic, environmental, and lifestyle factors. While personalized medicine holds great promise for improving treatment outcomes and patient satisfaction, it is essential to address challenges related to access, equity, and ethics to ensure that the benefits of personalized medicine are realized for all individuals. As the field continues to evolve, ongoing research and innovation will further enhance the ability to provide tailored and effective mental health care, ultimately advancing the goal of optimal mental well-being for every patient.

4

Integration of Mental and Physical Health Care

The integration of mental and physical health care represents a significant paradigm shift in the way healthcare systems approach patient well-being. Traditionally, mental health and physical health have been treated as distinct entities, often leading to fragmented care and suboptimal outcomes. However, emerging evidence and evolving practices are highlighting the benefits of a more integrated approach that addresses both mental and physical health simultaneously. This chapter explores the principles, models, and benefits of integrating mental and physical health care, along with the challenges and strategies for successful implementation.

At its core, the integration of mental and physical health care is based on the understanding that mental and physical health are intricately connected. Numerous studies have demonstrated that individuals with chronic physical conditions, such as diabetes, cardiovascular disease, or chronic pain, are at a higher risk of developing mental health issues, including depression and anxiety. Conversely, individuals with mental health conditions often experience worsened physical health outcomes and may struggle with managing chronic physical conditions. Recognizing this interplay underscores the importance of a holistic approach to care that considers both mental and physical aspects of health.

One of the foundational principles of integrated care is the concept of "whole-person care," which emphasizes treating the individual as a complete entity rather than focusing on isolated symptoms or conditions. This approach involves coordinating care across different providers and specialties to ensure that all aspects of a patient's health are addressed. Integrated care models aim to break down silos between mental health and primary care services, fostering collaboration and communication among healthcare professionals.

One effective model of integrated care is the "collaborative care" model. In this model, mental health professionals, such as psychologists or psychiatrists, work alongside primary care providers to deliver coordinated care. Collaborative care typically involves regular communication and case reviews between the mental health team and primary care providers, allowing for shared decision-making and treatment planning. This model often includes the use of evidence-based protocols and care pathways to ensure that patients receive comprehensive and effective care.

Another model is the "integrated behavioral health" approach, which involves embedding mental health services directly within primary care settings. In this model, mental health professionals are part of the primary care team and provide on-site assessment, treatment, and support. This integration facilitates early identification and intervention for mental health issues, reduces stigma associated with seeking mental health care, and enhances overall patient engagement. For example, a patient visiting a primary care clinic for a routine check-up might also receive a screening for depression or anxiety and have access to counseling services if needed.

The integration of mental and physical health care also involves the use of "patient-centered medical homes" (PCMH), which are healthcare delivery models designed to provide comprehensive, coordinated, and continuous care.

PCMHs focus on building strong patient-provider relationships and ensuring that care is tailored to individual needs. In a PCMH, mental health services are often incorporated into the care team, and care coordination is emphasized to address both mental and physical health needs. This model aims to improve the quality of care, enhance patient satisfaction, and reduce healthcare costs by providing a more holistic and coordinated approach.

One of the key benefits of integrating mental and physical health care is improved patient outcomes. Research has shown that integrated care models lead to better management of chronic physical conditions, reduced hospitalization rates, and improved mental health outcomes. For example, patients with diabetes who receive integrated care that includes mental health support are more likely to achieve better glycemic control and experience improved quality of life. Additionally, integrated care can enhance patient engagement and adherence to treatment plans, as patients receive more comprehensive and personalized care.

Despite the benefits, integrating mental and physical health care presents several challenges. One challenge is the need for effective communication and collaboration among healthcare providers. Different specialties often have their own approaches, terminologies, and workflows, which can create barriers to seamless coordination. Establishing clear communication channels and fostering a culture of collaboration are essential for overcoming these challenges and ensuring that care is well-coordinated.

Another challenge is the need for adequate training and support for healthcare professionals. Integrating mental and physical health care requires providers to have a broad understanding of both domains and the ability to work collaboratively with other professionals. Training programs and continuing education opportunities that emphasize integrated care principles and practices are crucial for equipping providers with the skills and knowledge needed to deliver effective care.

Furthermore, addressing systemic and organizational barriers is important for successful integration. This includes securing funding and resources to support integrated care initiatives, addressing regulatory and reimbursement issues, and developing policies that facilitate coordination between mental health and primary care services. Advocacy and policy efforts play a crucial role in promoting the integration of mental and physical health care and ensuring that it becomes a standard practice in healthcare systems.

In conclusion, the integration of mental and physical health care represents a transformative approach to healthcare that addresses the complex interplay between mental and physical health. By adopting models such as collaborative care, integrated behavioral health, and patient-centered medical homes, healthcare systems can provide more comprehensive, coordinated, and effective care. While challenges exist, including communication barriers, training needs, and systemic issues, the benefits of integrated care—improved patient outcomes, enhanced engagement, and better management of chronic conditions—make it a promising direction for the future of healthcare. As the field continues to evolve, ongoing efforts to overcome challenges and promote integration will be essential for advancing patient-centered and holistic care.

5

Innovations in Psychotherapy and Counseling

Psychotherapy and counseling are central to mental health care, offering individuals a means to address psychological issues, improve emotional well-being, and develop coping strategies. As mental health needs become increasingly complex and diverse, innovations in psychotherapy and counseling are emerging to enhance effectiveness, accessibility, and personalization of therapeutic interventions. This chapter explores several key innovations in the field, including advancements in therapeutic techniques, the integration of technology, and the evolution of therapeutic modalities.

One of the most significant innovations in psychotherapy is the development and refinement of evidence-based therapeutic techniques. Cognitive-behavioral therapy (CBT), which focuses on identifying and changing maladaptive thought patterns and behaviors, has long been a cornerstone of psychotherapy. Recent advancements have expanded the scope and applications of CBT, including the development of specialized forms such as mindfulness-based cognitive therapy (MBCT) and acceptance and commitment therapy (ACT). MBCT incorporates mindfulness practices to help individuals manage stress and prevent relapse in depression, while ACT emphasizes accepting difficult emotions and committing to values-based actions.

Another notable advancement in therapeutic techniques is the integration of trauma-informed care. Trauma-informed care recognizes the widespread impact of trauma on individuals' mental health and incorporates this understanding into therapeutic practice. This approach emphasizes creating a safe and supportive therapeutic environment, building trust, and empowering individuals to regain control over their lives. Trauma-informed care is particularly important for individuals with a history of abuse, neglect, or other traumatic experiences, and it helps ensure that therapy is sensitive to their unique needs and experiences.

The use of technology in psychotherapy and counseling is rapidly expanding, offering new tools and platforms for delivering therapeutic interventions. One of the most prominent technological innovations is the use of teletherapy, which allows therapists to conduct sessions remotely via video conferencing, phone calls, or chat-based applications. Teletherapy has become increasingly popular, particularly during the COVID-19 pandemic, as it provides a convenient and accessible option for individuals who may face barriers to in-person therapy. It also offers the flexibility to reach clients in remote or underserved areas, reducing geographical and logistical constraints.

In addition to teletherapy, digital mental health platforms and apps are transforming how individuals access and engage with therapeutic resources. These platforms often offer self-help tools, such as guided meditations, cognitive-behavioral exercises, and mood tracking, that complement traditional therapy. For instance, apps like Headspace and Calm provide mindfulness and relaxation techniques, while apps like Moodfit and Wysa offer tools for managing mood and emotional well-being. These digital tools can enhance therapy by providing ongoing support and resources outside of regular sessions, helping individuals practice and reinforce therapeutic skills.

Virtual reality (VR) and augmented reality (AR) are also emerging as innovative tools in psychotherapy. VR can create immersive environments for exposure therapy, allowing individuals to confront and manage fears or phobias in a controlled setting. For example, VR exposure therapy has been used effectively to treat post-traumatic stress disorder (PTSD) by simulating trauma-related scenarios in a safe environment. AR, which overlays digital information onto the real world, can enhance therapeutic experiences by providing interactive and engaging interventions. Both VR and AR offer novel ways to engage clients and provide therapeutic experiences that may be more impactful than traditional methods.

The evolution of therapeutic modalities includes the incorporation of integrative and holistic approaches that address the whole person rather than focusing solely on psychological symptoms. Integrative therapy combines elements from various therapeutic approaches, such as psychodynamic therapy, humanistic therapy, and behavioral therapy, to create a customized treatment plan tailored to the individual's needs. Holistic therapies, such as art therapy, music therapy, and dance/movement therapy, use creative and expressive methods to support emotional and psychological healing. These modalities recognize the importance of addressing multiple dimensions of an individual's experience and provide alternative ways to explore and express emotions.

Another important development in psychotherapy is the emphasis on culturally competent and inclusive practices. Culturally competent therapy acknowledges and respects the cultural, ethnic, and socioeconomic backgrounds of clients and integrates this understanding into the therapeutic process. This approach is essential for providing effective care to diverse populations and ensuring that therapy is relevant and sensitive to clients' unique cultural contexts. Culturally competent therapy involves understanding cultural norms, values, and experiences, and adapting therapeutic interventions to align with clients' cultural perspectives.

The rise of data-driven approaches and outcome measurement is also shaping the future of psychotherapy. By collecting and analyzing data on therapy outcomes, therapists can gain insights into the effectiveness of different interventions and tailor treatment plans accordingly. Outcome measurement tools, such as standardized assessments and client feedback surveys, help track progress and identify areas for improvement. Data-driven approaches support evidence-based practice and contribute to continuous improvement in therapeutic methods.

Despite these advancements, several challenges remain in the field of psychotherapy and counseling. Ensuring that innovative therapies are accessible and equitable for all individuals is a critical concern. Technological innovations, for example, may not be equally accessible to individuals with limited digital literacy or those in underserved areas. Additionally, the integration of new therapeutic techniques requires ongoing training and professional development for therapists to stay current with the latest advancements and best practices.

Ethical considerations are also important in the context of technological innovations and integrative approaches. Issues related to privacy, data security, and informed consent must be addressed to protect clients' rights and maintain the integrity of therapeutic relationships. As technology continues to evolve, it is essential to establish guidelines and standards that ensure the ethical use of digital tools and maintain the highest standards of care.

In conclusion, innovations in psychotherapy and counseling are expanding the horizons of mental health care by introducing new techniques, technologies, and modalities. From evidence-based therapeutic approaches to the integration of technology and holistic practices, these advancements are enhancing the effectiveness, accessibility, and personalization of therapy. While challenges exist, including ensuring equitable access and addressing ethical concerns, the ongoing development of innovative therapies holds promise for improving mental health care and supporting individuals in their journey toward emotional well-being. As the field continues to evolve, it will be essential to embrace and integrate these innovations while upholding the core principles of compassion, empathy, and respect in therapeutic practice.

6

The Impact of Social Media on Mental Health

Social media has become an integral part of modern life, profoundly influencing how people communicate, share information, and perceive themselves and others. Its impact on mental health is a topic of considerable debate and research, as social media platforms can both positively and negatively affect users' psychological well-being. This chapter explores the complex relationship between social media and mental health, examining how social media usage influences mental health outcomes, the mechanisms behind these effects, and strategies for mitigating potential risks.

One of the most prominent ways in which social media affects mental health is through its impact on self-esteem and body image. Platforms like Instagram, Facebook, and TikTok often feature curated and idealized representations of people's lives, bodies, and achievements. This can create unrealistic standards and contribute to feelings of inadequacy and low self-esteem among users. Research has shown that exposure to idealized images and posts can lead to body dissatisfaction and disordered eating behaviors, particularly among adolescents and young adults. The constant comparison to others' seemingly perfect lives can foster a sense of inferiority and contribute to mental health issues such as anxiety and depression.

Additionally, social media platforms can play a role in shaping and reinforcing identity and social belonging. For many users, social media provides a sense of community and connection, especially for those who may feel isolated in their offline lives. Online communities can offer support, validation, and a sense of belonging, which can be particularly beneficial for individuals with mental health conditions or those who are part of marginalized groups. Social media can facilitate connections with others who share similar experiences, interests, or challenges, providing a platform for mutual support and understanding.

However, the positive aspects of social media use are not without their potential drawbacks. The phenomenon of cyberbullying and online harassment is a significant concern, with many individuals experiencing negative interactions and abuse on social media platforms. Cyberbullying can have severe consequences for mental health, leading to increased stress, anxiety, and depression. The anonymity and reach of social media can amplify the impact of negative interactions, making it challenging for individuals to escape from harmful behavior.

The constant nature of social media engagement can also contribute to mental health issues such as stress and sleep disturbances. The pervasive presence of social media in everyday life means that users are often exposed to a continuous stream of notifications, updates, and messages. This can lead to information overload and heightened levels of stress, as individuals feel pressured to stay connected and respond promptly. Additionally, excessive use of social media, particularly before bedtime, can interfere with sleep patterns and contribute to insomnia. The blue light emitted by screens and the mental stimulation from engaging with social media can disrupt circadian rhythms and negatively impact sleep quality.

Social media platforms can also influence mental health through the spread of misinformation and the promotion of harmful behaviors. The rapid dissemination of unverified or misleading information can contribute to anxiety and confusion, particularly when it comes to health-related topics. Additionally, social media can sometimes perpetuate harmful trends or behaviors, such as self-harm or substance abuse, by exposing users to content that glorifies or normalizes these actions. The visibility of such content can potentially influence vulnerable individuals to engage in similar behaviors.

In response to these challenges, various strategies and interventions can help mitigate the negative impact of social media on mental health. Digital literacy education is crucial for empowering individuals to navigate social media in a healthy and informed manner. Teaching users about the potential risks of social media, promoting critical thinking, and encouraging the verification of information can help reduce the negative effects of misinformation and harmful content.

Implementing healthy social media habits is also essential for maintaining mental well-being. Setting boundaries around social media use, such as designated times for checking accounts and avoiding screens before bedtime, can help reduce stress and improve sleep quality. Encouraging users to engage in activities that promote positive mental health, such as physical exercise, mindfulness practices, and face-to-face social interactions, can counterbalance the negative effects of excessive social media use.

Additionally, social media platforms themselves have a role to play in addressing mental health concerns. Many platforms are increasingly recognizing the impact of their services on users' well-being and are taking steps to implement features that promote mental health. For example, some platforms have introduced tools for managing screen time, filtering out harmful content, and providing resources for mental health support. Collaboration between social media companies, mental health professionals, and policymakers is essential to ensure that these efforts are effective and that platforms prioritize user well-being.

In conclusion, social media has a multifaceted impact on mental health, with both positive and negative effects. While social media can provide opportunities for connection, support, and self-expression, it can also contribute to issues such as body dissatisfaction, cyberbullying, stress, and sleep disturbances. Understanding the complex relationship between social media and mental health is crucial for developing strategies to mitigate risks and promote healthy social media use. By fostering digital literacy, implementing healthy habits, and encouraging responsible platform practices, individuals and communities can better navigate the challenges of social media and support overall mental well-being. As social media continues to evolve, ongoing research and adaptation will be essential in addressing its impact on mental health and ensuring that its benefits are maximized while minimizing potential harms.

7

The Future of Mental Health Care: Emerging Trends and Technologies

The future of mental health care is being shaped by a confluence of emerging trends and technologies that promise to transform how mental health services are delivered, accessed, and experienced. As the field continues to evolve, new innovations and approaches are paving the way for more effective, personalized, and accessible mental health care. This chapter explores several key trends and technologies that are poised to influence the future of mental health care, including advancements in digital health, the integration of artificial intelligence, and the development of novel therapeutic approaches.

One of the most significant trends in mental health care is the increasing integration of digital health technologies. Digital health encompasses a range of tools and platforms designed to support mental health and well-being through technology. This includes teletherapy, mental health apps, and digital self-help resources. Teletherapy has become a widely adopted modality, particularly in response to the COVID-19 pandemic, providing individuals with the convenience of remote access to mental health professionals. As technology continues to advance, teletherapy platforms are likely to offer even more features, such as enhanced video quality, secure messaging, and integrated therapeutic tools.

Mental health apps have also gained popularity as a means of providing accessible and cost-effective support. These apps offer a variety of features, including mood tracking, cognitive-behavioral exercises, guided meditation, and symptom monitoring. Examples include apps like Calm, Headspace, and Moodfit, which provide users with tools to manage stress, anxiety, and depression. The proliferation of mental health apps reflects a growing recognition of the need for on-demand support and self-management options. As these apps become more sophisticated, they may incorporate additional functionalities, such as personalized feedback, AI-driven insights, and integration with wearable devices.

Wearable technology is another area of growth in digital health. Wearables, such as smartwatches and fitness trackers, can monitor physiological indicators like heart rate, sleep patterns, and physical activity. These devices can provide valuable data for understanding and managing mental health conditions. For example, wearable devices that track sleep patterns can help individuals with insomnia or mood disorders identify patterns and triggers related to their condition. As wearable technology advances, it is expected to offer even more precise and actionable insights into mental health and well-being.

Artificial intelligence (AI) and machine learning are transforming mental health care by enhancing diagnostic accuracy, personalizing treatment, and improving decision-making. AI algorithms can analyze large datasets, including electronic health records, genetic information, and neuroimaging data, to identify patterns and predict outcomes. For instance, AI-powered tools can assist in diagnosing mental health conditions by analyzing speech patterns, facial expressions, and behavioral data. These tools can support clinicians in making more accurate diagnoses and developing individualized treatment plans.

Machine learning models can also be used to predict treatment responses and optimize therapeutic interventions. By analyzing data from previous patients, AI algorithms can identify which treatments are most likely to be effective for a given individual based on their unique profile. This personalized approach can help reduce the trial-and-error process in finding the right treatment and improve overall outcomes. Additionally, AI-driven chatbots and virtual therapists are emerging as tools for providing support and guidance in real-time. These AI-powered systems can offer psychoeducation, coping strategies, and even therapeutic interventions, complementing traditional therapy and expanding access to mental health resources.

The development of novel therapeutic approaches is another key trend in the future of mental health care. One such approach is psychedelic-assisted therapy, which involves the use of substances like psilocybin, MDMA, or ketamine in conjunction with psychotherapy. Research has shown that these substances can have profound effects on mood, cognition, and emotional processing, potentially offering new avenues for treating conditions like depression, PTSD, and anxiety. Clinical trials are ongoing to assess the safety and efficacy of psychedelic-assisted therapy, and it is anticipated that these treatments may become an integral part of mental health care in the future.

Another innovative approach is neurofeedback, a form of biofeedback that uses real-time monitoring of brain activity to help individuals regulate their mental states. Neurofeedback involves placing sensors on the scalp to measure brainwaves and providing feedback through visual or auditory cues. This technique has shown promise in treating conditions such as ADHD, anxiety, and depression by helping individuals learn to modulate their brain activity and improve emotional regulation. As technology advances, neurofeedback systems are likely to become more accessible and effective, offering personalized interventions for a range of mental health conditions.

The future of mental health care will also be influenced by advances in genomics and personalized medicine. As our understanding of the genetic and epigenetic factors contributing to mental health conditions grows, personalized approaches to treatment are likely to become more prevalent. Genomic research can identify genetic markers associated with mental health disorders and inform the development of targeted therapies. For example, pharmacogenomic testing can help determine how an individual's genetic makeup influences their response to medications, leading to more precise and effective treatment plans.

Moreover, the integration of mental health care with primary care and other healthcare services is expected to become more seamless. Integrated care models that combine mental health and physical health services can provide a more holistic approach to patient care. This integration involves coordinating care across different providers and specialties, ensuring that mental health and physical health needs are addressed in a unified manner. Collaborative care models, patient-centered medical homes, and interdisciplinary teams are examples of approaches that support integrated mental health care and improve overall health outcomes.

As these trends and technologies continue to evolve, it is important to address the ethical, regulatory, and practical challenges associated with their implementation. Issues related to data privacy, informed consent, and equitable access to innovative treatments must be carefully managed to ensure that the benefits of these advancements are realized while protecting patient rights and promoting fairness. Additionally, ongoing research and evaluation are essential to assess the effectiveness and safety of new technologies and approaches.

In conclusion, the future of mental health care is being shaped by a range of emerging trends and technologies that offer the potential for significant improvements in diagnosis, treatment, and access to care. Digital health innovations, AI and machine learning, novel therapeutic approaches, and personalized medicine are all contributing to a more dynamic and effective mental health care landscape. As these advancements continue to develop, they hold the promise of enhancing the quality of care, increasing accessibility, and improving outcomes for individuals with mental health conditions. By embracing these innovations and addressing associated challenges, the mental health care field can advance toward a future of more personalized, integrated, and impactful care.

8

Mental Health and the Workplace: Emerging Strategies for Support

The workplace is a critical environment that can significantly influence employees' mental health and overall well-being. With increasing recognition of the impact of mental health on productivity, job satisfaction, and organizational success, employers are investing in new strategies and initiatives to support mental health in the workplace. This chapter explores emerging strategies for mental health support at work, including comprehensive wellness programs, mental health training, policy development, and the role of leadership in fostering a supportive work environment.

One of the most effective strategies for supporting mental health in the workplace is the implementation of comprehensive wellness programs. These programs are designed to promote overall well-being and include a range of services and initiatives such as employee assistance programs (EAPs), mental health resources, and wellness activities. EAPs provide confidential counseling, support, and resources for employees dealing with personal or work-related issues. These services can include stress management, financial counseling, and referrals to mental health professionals. By offering EAPs, employers can provide immediate support and resources to help employees address mental health concerns before they escalate.

In addition to EAPs, wellness programs may include activities and initiatives that promote mental health, such as mindfulness workshops, fitness classes, and relaxation areas. Mindfulness and stress reduction techniques, such as meditation and yoga, can help employees manage stress and improve their overall mental well-being. Fitness classes and exercise programs contribute to physical health, which is closely linked to mental health. Creating spaces for relaxation and social interaction, such as break rooms or quiet areas, can also enhance employees' mental well-being by providing opportunities for rest and rejuvenation.

Mental health training and education are crucial components of workplace mental health strategies. Training programs for managers and employees can increase awareness of mental health issues, reduce stigma, and provide practical tools for supporting colleagues. Managerial training often focuses on recognizing signs of mental health struggles, offering support, and creating an inclusive environment. For example, training may cover how to approach conversations about mental health, how to accommodate employees' needs, and how to provide constructive feedback without exacerbating stress.

Employee training programs may include workshops on stress management, resilience building, and work-life balance. Educating employees about mental health and providing them with skills to manage their own well-being can empower them to take proactive steps to maintain mental health and seek help when needed. By fostering a culture of learning and awareness, organizations can create an environment where mental health is openly discussed and supported.

Policy development is another key strategy for supporting mental health in the workplace. Establishing clear policies and procedures related to mental health can help create a supportive and equitable work environment. Policies may include provisions for mental health leave, accommodations for employees with mental health conditions, and procedures for reporting and addressing mental health concerns. Ensuring that policies are inclusive and non-discriminatory is essential for promoting fairness and accessibility.

For example, policies that provide paid sick leave or flexible working arrangements can help employees manage mental health conditions without facing financial or professional penalties. Accommodations such as modified work schedules or remote work options can support employees in balancing their mental health needs with job responsibilities. Clearly communicated policies and procedures can also help employees understand their rights and available resources, reducing barriers to accessing support.

Leadership plays a pivotal role in shaping the culture and practices related to mental health in the workplace. Leaders who prioritize mental health and demonstrate a commitment to creating a supportive work environment can influence organizational culture and employee attitudes. Leadership can impact mental health support through their actions, communication, and decision-making.

Leaders who openly discuss mental health and model healthy behaviors set a positive example for employees. By sharing their own experiences, acknowledging the importance of mental health, and participating in wellness initiatives, leaders can help normalize conversations about mental health and reduce stigma. Additionally, leaders can advocate for and invest in mental health resources, ensuring that adequate support is available and accessible to employees.

Creating a supportive work environment also involves promoting work-life balance and addressing factors that contribute to employee stress and burnout. Strategies for promoting work-life balance may include offering flexible work arrangements, encouraging regular breaks, and setting realistic expectations for workloads. Addressing workplace stressors, such as excessive overtime, high demands, and lack of support, is essential for preventing burnout and promoting long-term mental health.

Measuring and evaluating the effectiveness of mental health initiatives is an important aspect of developing and refining workplace strategies. Collecting data through employee surveys, feedback, and health metrics can provide insights into the impact of mental health programs and identify areas for improvement. Regular evaluation allows organizations to adjust their strategies based on employee needs and experiences, ensuring that mental health support remains relevant and effective.

Challenges in implementing mental health strategies in the workplace include addressing resistance to change, managing costs, and ensuring accessibility for all employees. Overcoming resistance to mental health initiatives may require addressing misconceptions, engaging stakeholders, and demonstrating the benefits of investing in mental health. Managing costs involves balancing budget constraints with the need for comprehensive support, while ensuring accessibility requires addressing diverse needs and barriers faced by employees from different backgrounds.

In conclusion, emerging strategies for mental health support in the workplace reflect a growing recognition of the importance of mental well-being for overall organizational success. Comprehensive wellness programs, mental health training, policy development, and leadership are key components of a holistic approach to workplace mental health. By investing in these strategies and addressing associated challenges, organizations can create a supportive and inclusive environment that promotes mental health, enhances employee well-being, and contributes to a positive and productive workplace culture. As the field of workplace mental health continues to evolve, ongoing innovation and commitment will be essential for advancing mental health support and achieving meaningful outcomes for employees and organizations alike.

9

The Role of Community in Mental Health: Building Supportive Networks

Community plays a vital role in shaping mental health outcomes, providing individuals with a sense of belonging, support, and resources that can significantly impact their well-being. The influence of community on mental health extends beyond individual interactions to encompass the collective social, cultural, and environmental factors that contribute to mental wellness. This chapter delves into the multifaceted role of community in mental health, exploring the ways in which community networks, social support systems, and collective resources contribute to mental well-being and offering strategies for building and enhancing supportive communities.

One of the primary ways in which community affects mental health is through the provision of social support. Social support encompasses the emotional, informational, and practical assistance provided by friends, family, and other social networks. This support can help individuals cope with stress, navigate challenges, and improve their overall mental health. Research has shown that strong social support is associated with lower levels of anxiety, depression, and psychological distress. Communities that foster close-knit relationships and provide opportunities for social interaction can enhance individuals' sense of belonging and reduce feelings of isolation.

Supportive communities often include formal and informal networks that offer assistance and resources. Formal networks may include community organizations, mental health services, and support groups that provide targeted help for specific issues or conditions. For example, community centers may offer counseling services, workshops on mental health, and support groups for individuals experiencing similar challenges. Informal networks, such as neighborhood groups, faith communities, and social clubs, can also provide valuable support through shared activities, companionship, and mutual assistance.

The concept of social capital is integral to understanding the role of community in mental health. Social capital refers to the resources and benefits derived from social networks, including trust, reciprocity, and social cohesion. High levels of social capital are associated with improved mental health outcomes, as individuals in communities with strong social ties and a sense of mutual support are more likely to experience positive mental well-being. Building and nurturing social capital involves fostering relationships, promoting community engagement, and creating opportunities for individuals to connect and contribute to their communities.

Community environments also play a significant role in shaping mental health. The physical and social characteristics of a community, such as access to green spaces, safe and supportive neighborhoods, and quality housing, can influence mental well-being. Research has shown that living in environments with access to parks, recreational areas, and safe walking routes is associated with lower levels of stress and improved mental health. Communities that prioritize creating healthy and supportive environments can enhance residents' overall well-being and contribute to a higher quality of life.

Addressing mental health disparities and promoting inclusivity is an important aspect of building supportive communities. Marginalized and underserved populations may face additional barriers to accessing mental health resources and experiencing social support. To create inclusive communities, it is essential to address systemic inequalities, provide culturally competent services, and ensure that mental health support is accessible to all individuals, regardless of their background or socioeconomic status. Initiatives such as community outreach programs, language services, and culturally tailored support can help bridge gaps and promote mental health equity.

Community-based mental health initiatives can also play a critical role in prevention and early intervention. By promoting mental health awareness and providing educational resources, communities can help individuals recognize early signs of mental health issues and seek support before problems escalate. Community workshops, public awareness campaigns, and school-based programs can contribute to reducing stigma and increasing knowledge about mental health. Early intervention efforts, such as providing support to at-risk youth or offering mental health screenings in community settings, can help address issues proactively and improve overall community mental health.

Creating and sustaining supportive communities requires active participation and collaboration from various stakeholders, including community leaders, organizations, and residents. Engaging community members in the development and implementation of mental health initiatives ensures that programs are relevant, effective, and responsive to local needs. Collaborative approaches, such as partnerships between mental health organizations, schools, businesses, and local government, can leverage resources and expertise to address mental health challenges comprehensively.

Involving community members in decision-making processes and encouraging their input can enhance the effectiveness of mental health initiatives. For example, community advisory boards or focus groups can provide valuable feedback on the design and delivery of mental health programs, ensuring that they align with community values and preferences. Empowering individuals to take an active role in their communities fosters a sense of ownership and investment in mental health efforts, contributing to more sustainable and impactful outcomes.

Challenges in building supportive communities for mental health include overcoming resistance to change, addressing resource limitations, and navigating diverse needs and preferences. Resistance to mental health initiatives may arise due to stigma, lack of awareness, or conflicting priorities. To address these challenges, it is important to engage in open dialogue, provide education, and demonstrate the benefits of mental health support. Resource limitations, such as funding constraints or inadequate infrastructure, can be addressed through creative solutions, such as leveraging volunteers, seeking grants, and forming partnerships with other organizations.

Navigating diverse needs and preferences requires a flexible and inclusive approach. Recognizing the unique experiences and cultural backgrounds of community members and tailoring mental health initiatives to address these differences is essential for promoting inclusivity and effectiveness. Additionally, ongoing evaluation and feedback mechanisms can help identify areas for improvement and ensure that programs remain relevant and responsive to evolving community needs.

In conclusion, the role of community in mental health is profound and multifaceted, encompassing social support, environmental factors, and collective resources. By fostering strong social networks, creating supportive environments, and addressing mental health disparities, communities can play a crucial role in enhancing mental well-being and promoting overall quality of life. Building and sustaining supportive communities requires active participation, collaboration, and a commitment to inclusivity and equity. As communities continue to evolve, ongoing efforts to strengthen social ties, provide resources, and address mental health challenges will be essential for creating environments that support and nurture the mental health of all individuals.

10

Epilogue: Embracing the Future of Mental Health Care

As we conclude this exploration of the future of mental health care, it is essential to reflect on the profound transformations taking place in the field and the opportunities that lie ahead. The journey through the chapters has illuminated the dynamic landscape of mental health care, highlighting emerging trends, innovative technologies, and evolving strategies that promise to redefine how we understand and address mental health challenges. This epilogue aims to synthesize these insights, emphasize the importance of continued progress, and inspire a vision for a more inclusive and effective mental health care system.

The landscape of mental health care is undergoing a profound shift, driven by advancements in technology, growing awareness of mental health issues, and a greater emphasis on holistic and personalized approaches. Digital health tools, such as teletherapy, mental health apps, and wearable devices, have expanded access to care and empowered individuals to take control of their mental health. The integration of artificial intelligence and machine learning is enhancing diagnostic accuracy, personalizing treatment, and providing real-time support. These innovations are not merely technical advancements; they represent a fundamental change in how mental health care is delivered and experienced, making it more accessible, responsive, and tailored to individual needs.

One of the key themes emerging from this exploration is the importance of integration and collaboration. The future of mental health care relies on the seamless integration of various services and disciplines, including primary care, mental health services, and community support. Integrated care models that address both mental and physical health needs holistically are essential for providing comprehensive and effective support. Collaboration among mental health professionals, healthcare providers, community organizations, and policymakers is crucial for developing and implementing strategies that address the complex and multifaceted nature of mental health.

The role of community in mental health care has been a central focus, emphasizing the need for supportive networks and environments. Communities play a vital role in providing social support, fostering inclusivity, and addressing disparities. Building strong, supportive communities involves creating spaces where individuals feel connected, valued, and understood. It also requires addressing systemic issues and ensuring that mental health resources are accessible to all. The power of community lies in its ability to provide a sense of belonging and collective resilience, which can significantly impact mental well-being.

The integration of mental health into workplace environments has also emerged as a critical area for development. The recognition of mental health as an integral component of overall well-being has led to the implementation of innovative strategies, including comprehensive wellness programs, mental health training, and supportive policies. These initiatives reflect a growing understanding of the impact of mental health on productivity, job satisfaction, and organizational success. As workplaces continue to evolve, it is essential to prioritize mental health and create environments that support employees' well-being.

EPILOGUE: EMBRACING THE FUTURE OF MENTAL HEALTH CARE

Looking ahead, the future of mental health care will be shaped by ongoing research, technological advancements, and evolving societal attitudes. Continued investment in research is vital for understanding the underlying causes of mental health conditions, developing new treatments, and improving outcomes. Technological innovations will continue to play a significant role, offering new tools and approaches for diagnosis, treatment, and support. As we embrace these advancements, it is essential to ensure that they are implemented ethically and equitably, addressing issues such as data privacy, accessibility, and inclusivity.

Moreover, the importance of maintaining a human-centered approach cannot be overstated. While technology and innovation are transforming mental health care, the core of effective mental health support lies in empathy, understanding, and meaningful human connections. The integration of technology should enhance, not replace, the human elements of care. Building relationships with mental health professionals, accessing support through community networks, and engaging in self-care practices are all integral to achieving and maintaining mental well-being.

As we move forward, it is crucial to continue advocating for mental health awareness, reducing stigma, and promoting mental health as a fundamental aspect of overall health. Public awareness campaigns, educational initiatives, and advocacy efforts are essential for creating a culture that prioritizes mental health and supports individuals in seeking help. By fostering an environment where mental health is openly discussed and valued, we can contribute to a more compassionate and supportive society.

In conclusion, the future of mental health care holds immense promise, driven by innovation, collaboration, and a commitment to holistic well-being. The advancements and strategies explored in this book represent a significant step forward in addressing mental health challenges and improving the quality of care. Embracing these developments while maintaining a focus on empathy, inclusivity, and human connection will be key to creating a mental health care system that is effective, equitable, and supportive. As we continue to advance and evolve, let us remain committed to the vision of a future where mental health is prioritized, support is accessible, and every individual has the opportunity to thrive.

www.ingramcontent.com/pod-product-compliance
Lightning Source LLC
Chambersburg PA
CBHW072326020225
21301CB00011B/1201